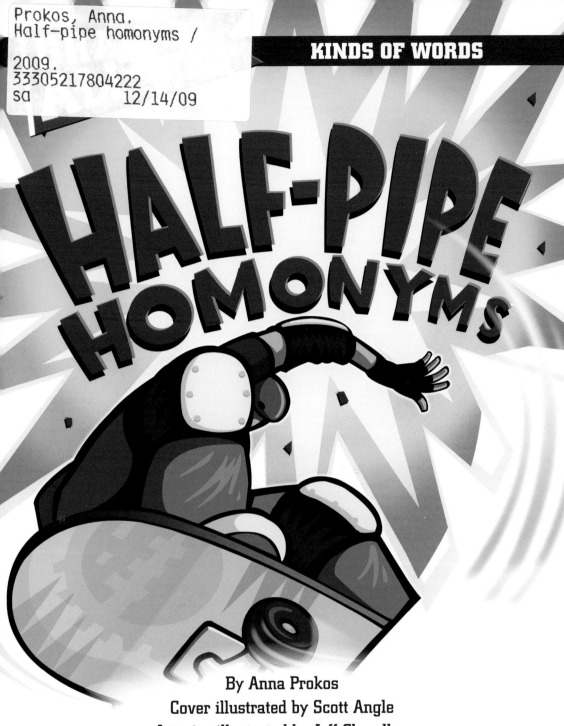

HALF-PIPE HOMONYMS

By Anna Prokos
Cover illustrated by Scott Angle
Interior illustrated by Jeff Chandler
Language arts curriculum consultant: Debra Voege, M.A.

Gareth Stevens
Publishing

Please visit our web site at **www.garethstevens.com**.
For a free color catalog describing Gareth Stevens Publishing's list of
high-quality books , call 1-800-542-2595 (USA) or 1-800-387-3178 (Canada).
Gareth Stevens Publishing's fax: 1-877-542-2596

Library of Congress Cataloging-in-Publication Data

Prokos, Anna.
      Half-pipe homonyms / by Anna Prokos ; illustrated by Scott Angle ;
language arts curriculum consultant: Debra Voege.
          p. cm. — (Grammar all-stars : kinds of words)
      At head of title : Grammar all-stars : kinds of words
      Includes bibliographical references and index.
      ISBN-10: 1-4339-0010-6   ISBN-13: 978-1-4339-0010-5 (lib. bdg.)
      ISBN-10: 1-4339-0150-1   ISBN-13: 978-1-4339-0150-8 (pbk.)
      1. English language—Homonyms—Juvenile literature. 2. English
language—Grammar—Juvenile literature. I. Angle, Scott. II. Voege, Debra.
III. Title. IV. Title: Grammar all-stars : kinds of words.
PE1595.P76   2008
428.1—dc22   2008027625

This edition first published in 2009 by
Gareth Stevens Publishing
A Weekly Reader® Company
1 Reader's Digest Road
Pleasantville, NY 10570-7000 USA

Copyright © 2009 by Gareth Stevens, Inc.

Executive Managing Editor: Lisa M. Herrington
Senior Editor: Barbara Bakowski
Creative Director: Lisa Donovan
Art Director: Ken Crossland
Publisher: Keith Garton

Printed in the United States of America

1 2 3 4 5 6 7 8 9 10 09 08

CONTENTS

Look for the **boldface** words on each page.
Then read the **HALF-PIPE HINT** that follows.

CHAPTER 1

AIR TIME

What Are Homonyms?

"**Hi**! Buzz Star **here** for P-L-A-Y TV. I'm at the Big Air **Jam**," Buzz says, looking into a camera. "This place is really jamming!"

A girl enters the broadcast booth. "You **mean** it's *wheely* jamming!" she says. "I'm sorry **for** interrupting, but I've always wanted to **be** a reporter."

Buzz smiles. "I'd be *wheely* honored if you helped me today," he replies. "Folks, **meet** Mayumi Miyaki. She's a youth skateboarding champ!"

"Please call me **May**. Everyone does," she says.

"OK, May. How old were you when you started skateboarding?" Buzz asks.

"My tenth birthday is next month, and I've been skating for about **two** years. **So** I must have been **eight** years old," May replies.

"**There** are a lot of homonyms in **your** answer," Buzz says.

"What are homonyms?" asks May.

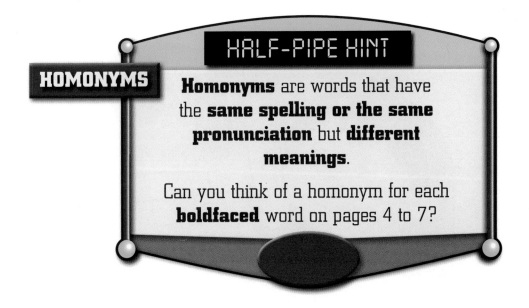

HALF-PIPE HINT

HOMONYMS

Homonyms are words that have the **same spelling or the same pronunciation** but **different meanings**.

Can you think of a homonym for each **boldfaced** word on pages 4 to 7?

"Homonyms are words that have the same spelling or the same pronunciation but different meanings," answers Buzz. "The word **may** is a type of homonym called a homograph. **May** can be the name of a month or the name of a girl. It can also mean *have permission to*."

"Oh, I see!" May says. "Are **see** and **sea** homographs?"

"No, **see** and **sea** are homophones. Homophones are another kind of homonym," Buzz explains. "They sound the same but have different spellings and meanings."

"Thanks for the language lesson, Buzz," says May. "You know a lot about homonyms!"

CHAPTER 2

SOUNDS LIKE SUPER STUNTS!

What Are Homophones?

"With you helping me describe the action today, May, **our** viewers won't be **bored**!" says Buzz.

"I am excited about watching this event—and competing, **too**," May says. "I've practiced my **board** tricks for **two** whole years. In less than an **hour**, I'll be trying one of the hardest moves in the sport."

"That's great to **hear**! May, tell the P-L-A-Y TV viewers what you and the other skateboarders will do **here** today."

Homophones are a kind of homonym. Homophones are words that **sound alike** but are **spelled differently** and have **different meanings**.

Example: bored = uninterested
board = piece of wood

I hope I can nail this!

May points to a U-shaped ramp. "That is a half-pipe," she explains. "**It's** made out of **wood**. The skaters **would** normally perform **their** stunts and tricks **there**," May explains.

"**They're** going to skate on that?" Buzz says. "**Its** shape looks dangerous to me."

"A half-pipe can be dangerous. Skateboarders **wear** protective gear," May points out.

"Staying safe is important," Buzz agrees. "Now **where** is my notebook?"

"I haven't seen **your** book, Buzz," May says. "Why do you need it?"

"I want to **write** down that safety rule," Buzz replies.

"Skip the notes. The Big Air Jam is starting!" May exclaims.

"**You're** absolutely **right**, May," Buzz says. "Let's jam!"

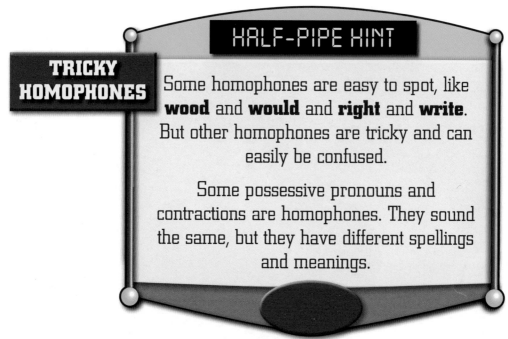

HALF-PIPE HINT

TRICKY HOMOPHONES

Some homophones are easy to spot, like **wood** and **would** and **right** and **write**. But other homophones are tricky and can easily be confused.

Some possessive pronouns and contractions are homophones. They sound the same, but they have different spellings and meanings.

CHAPTER 3

ON A ROLL

What Are Homographs?

May and Buzz turn their gaze to the skating area. "What time is it?" May asks.

Buzz glances at his **watch**. "Eleven o'clock," he replies.

"I have time to **watch** a few of the other skateboarders," May says. "There's Ricky Ramp. He is one of the sport's biggest stars. He has thousands of **fans**."

"Speaking of **fans**, we have a few of them blowing in the broadcast booth. The temperature is rising today!" Buzz says.

"The temperature isn't the only thing that's going up," Buzz says. "Look! Ricky Ramp is doing a handstand at the **top** of the half-pipe!"

"That trick is called an invert," May says. "I tried it once, but I slammed into the **hard** floor of the half-pipe. Good thing I was wearing my helmet!"

"It will be **hard** to **top** Ricky's performance," Buzz says.

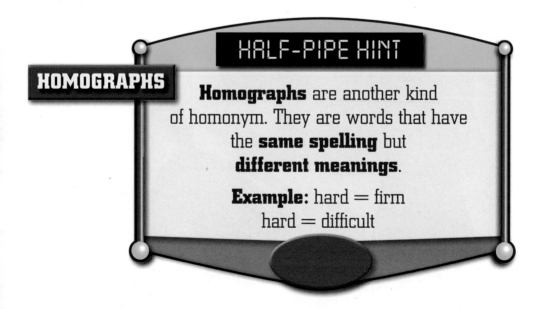

HALF-PIPE HINT

HOMOGRAPHS

Homographs are another kind of homonym. They are words that have the **same spelling** but **different meanings**.

Example: hard = firm
hard = difficult

After Ricky **leaves** the half-pipe, he **heads** over to talk to Buzz and May. They **move** to make room for him in the broadcast booth.

"Ricky Ramp is joining us, folks," Buzz says. "That invert was quite a **move**, Ricky! Do you have any advice for our viewers who might want to give it a try?"

"It's important to stay safe," Ricky replies. "I hope your viewers always wear a helmet so they don't hurt their **heads**!"

"That's a good reminder," Buzz says with a nod. "Ricky, tell us what it is like at the top of the half-pipe."

"I can see the **leaves** on the treetops," Ricky replies. "It's awesome!"

"**Duck**!" May shouts.

"No, I didn't see a **duck** up there,"
Ricky says, looking confused. "But I did see
a lot of other birds."

"She means DUCK!" Buzz grabs Ricky's
arm and pulls the skater to the floor. "A
flying skateboard is coming this way!"

Ollie Oops runs toward the booth. "Are you OK?" he asks.

"Not a scratch on us," Buzz answers. "Folks, this is Ollie Oops, a pro who **rolls** at top speed. Thanks for joining us, Ollie."

"I just came by to bring May a sandwich," Ollie says.

"Where's *my* lunch?" Buzz asks.

"Don't worry, dude," Ollie replies. "I've got enough **rolls** for everyone."

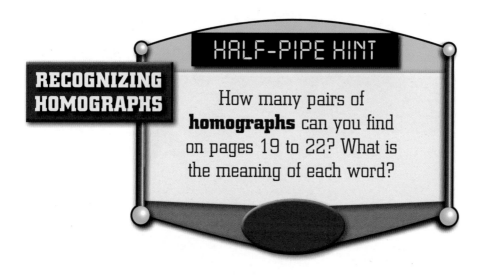

RECOGNIZING HOMOGRAPHS

HALF-PIPE HINT

How many pairs of **homographs** can you find on pages 19 to 22? What is the meaning of each word?

Ollie hands Buzz a sandwich.

"Folks, we'll be back after a message from our sponsors," Buzz says. As soon as he is off the air, he takes a big bite.

May turns to Ricky Ramp. "It's time for me to skate. Can you take over for me on TV, Ricky?"

"I'd like to help, but I'm taking my little brother to the circus this afternoon," Ricky says. "It's my birthday **present** to him."

"I can fill in," Ollie says. "I'd be happy to **present** the Big Air Jam with Buzz."

"Good luck!" Buzz tells May. "Go take the **lead** in this competition!"

"I feel nervous," May says. "My legs feel as if they are made of **lead**."

"You'll be fine," Buzz assures her. He leans **close** to May's ear and speaks softly. "Just **close** your eyes and take a deep breath. Then have some fun!"

Buzz gets the signal that he is back on the air. "For those viewers who are just tuning in, I'm reporting **live** from the Big Air Jam," Buzz says. "Next up is young May Miyaki. She and her family **live** nearby. May will try one of the hardest tricks on the half-pipe: the 900."

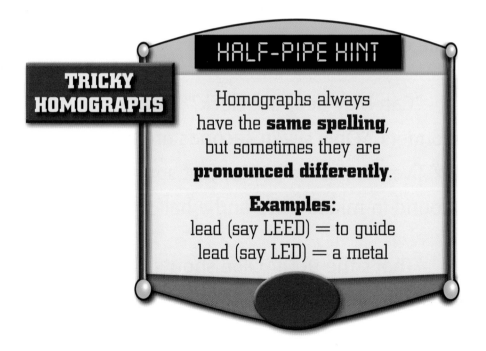

TRICKY HOMOGRAPHS

HALF-PIPE HINT

Homographs always have the **same spelling**, but sometimes they are **pronounced differently**.

Examples:
lead (say LEED) = to guide
lead (say LED) = a metal

"That's one sick stunt!" Ollie adds. "At last month's Battle of the Boards, May busted some really rad tricks, like a McTwist and a rocket air. She skates goofy."

"That's not a very nice thing to say!" Buzz scolds.

"No, dude! *Goofy* means she skates with her left foot on the tail of the board," Ollie explains.

"Can May beat the clock?" Buzz wonders. "Only seven seconds are left. Six, five, four ... Wow! May just spun around in midair—two and a half times!"

"That's the 900!" Ollie shouts. "She did it! Way to go, May!"

The crowd cheers wildly as May makes her way back to the broadcast booth. "Congratulations, May!" Buzz says. "Were you nervous as time began to **wind** down?"

"At first I was scared," May admits. "But then I felt the **wind** in my hair, and I just knew I could land the 900!"

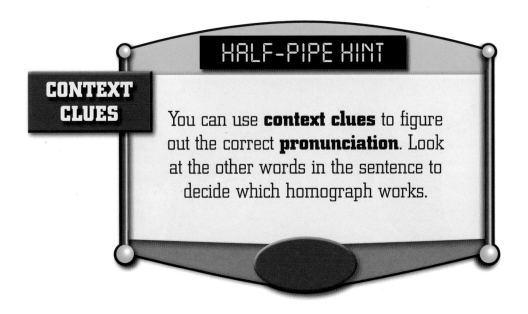

HALF-PIPE HINT

CONTEXT CLUES

You can use **context clues** to figure out the correct **pronunciation**. Look at the other words in the sentence to decide which homograph works.

"That performance has earned you a trophy. You are the youngest winner of the Big Air Jam!" Buzz faces the camera. "This is Buzz Star, signing off! Until next time, keep on rolling!"

Homophones are words that sound alike but are spelled differently and have different meanings.

Example: see (to view) and **sea** (ocean)

To remember what **homophones** are, break the word into two parts: *homo* ("same") and *phone* ("sound"). Homophones sound the same.

Sometimes, **homophones** are tricky. Some possessive pronouns and contractions sound the same, but they have different spellings and different meanings.

Possessive Pronoun	**Contraction**
its: belonging to it	**it's:** it is
your: belonging to you	**you're:** you are
their: belonging to them	**they're:** they are

Context clues can help you use **homophones** correctly. Look at the other words in the sentence to decide which homophone works.

Homographs are words that are spelled the same but have different meanings.

Example: watch (timepiece) and **watch** (to look at)

To remember what **homographs** are, break the word into two parts: *homo* ("same") and *graph* ("write"). Homographs are written the same way.

Homographs always have the same spelling, but sometimes they are pronounced differently. Use context clues to figure out how to say the word.

Example: May waits for the clock to **wind** down. She takes off her helmet and feels the **wind** in her hair.

May wrote an article about the Big Air Jam for her local newspaper. On a piece of paper, **list 20 incorrect homophones** in May's article.

Sore Into Action!

By Mayumi Mayaki

This weak, thousands of skateboarding *fans* came to *watch* the Big Air Jam contest. Viewers could sea announcer Buzz Star and me *live* on P-L-A-Y TV. I skated in the half-pipe event, two, sew Ollie Oops filled in four me briefly.

I new the Big Air Jam wood knot bee boring. Their were ate skateboarders. The first skater was Ricky Ramp. He wowed the crowd!

Then I skated on the half-pipe. I had to decide witch tricks to due. I wanted to take the *lead*. I did won of the toughest stunts in skateboarding: the 900. I could feel the *wind* in my hare. I landed write wear I was supposed to. The hole crowd went wild! I one a big trophy. It was a day I'll never forget!

All-Star Challenge

The words in *italic* type are *homographs*. On a piece of paper, list the 5 homographs in May's article. Write two meanings for each word.

Turn the page to check your answers and to see how many points you scored!

ANSWER KEY

Did you find enough homophones to heat up the half-pipe?

0–5 homophones: Ollie

6–10 homophones: Kickflip

11–15 homophones: McTwist

16–20 homophones: THE 900!

HOMOPHONES

1. Sore → Soar
2. weak → week
3. sea → see
4. two → too
5. sew → so
6. four → for
7. new → knew
8. wood → would
9. knot → not
10. bee → be
11. Their → There
12. ate → eight
13. witch → which
14. due → do
15. won → one
16. hare → hair
17. write → right
18. wear → where
19. hole → whole
20. one → won

 **All-Star Challenge**

1. *fans:* enthusiasts **OR** machines that blow air
2. *watch:* to look at **OR** a timepiece
3. *live:* to be alive **OR** broadcast at the same time
4. *lead:* position at the front **OR** a kind of metal
5. *wind:* moving air **OR** to turn a spring